Contents

Foreword: 4

Book One: Muffin Tin Menus 6

   Breakfast Muffins 7

   Lasagna Bites – Version 1 10

   Lasagna Bites – Version 2 13

   Parmesan Spinach Bites 16

   Stuffed Chicken Breast 19

   Chicken Taco Cups 22

   Mini Meatloaves 25

   Muffin Cup Corn Dogs 28

   Handheld Hash Brown Casseroles 31

   with REAL Apples 34

   Mini Quiche 38

   Portion-Perfect Frittatas 41

   Asian Dumplings 45

   Mini Pizzas 49

   Frozen Fruit Treats 52

   Two-Bite French Toast 54

   Handheld Bacon and Eggs 58

   Mini Chicken Pot Pie 61

Book Two: Muffin Tin Madness 64

Morning Sunrise Muffins 65

Homemade Breakfast Sandwiches 69

Dreamy Pineapple 72

Coconut Pies 72

Portion-Perfect Crab Cakes 77

Sinfully Simple Chocolate Lava Cupcakes 80

Gourmet Lava Cakes 84

with Mocha Sauce 84

Mini Greek Pizzas 90

Monkey Bread 94

Cranberry Brie Puffs 98

Mushroom Brie Tarts 100

Cheddar Sausage Biscuits 104

Spinach and Feta Bites 108

Mini Pineapple 112

Upside-Down Cakes 112

Mini Pumpkin Pie 115

Handy and Hardy 118

Shepherd's Pies 118

Piping Hot Dippin' Burgers 121

Mini Turkey Meatloaf 126

Choco-Nana Bread Pudding 130

Book Three: Muffin Tin Cuisine 134

Mac n Cheese Mouthfuls	135
Danish Delights	139
Pancake Fruit Cups	142
Yogurt-Filled Granola Cups	147
Maple Sausage Pancake Bites	151
PB&J Muffins	154
Mashed Potato Bake	157
Calzones	160
Bacon-Wrapped	164
Egg Scramble	164
No-Bake Mini Cheesecakes	167
Eggplant Parmesan	170
Ham and Egg Breakfast	175
Fish Tacos	178
French Toast Bowls	183
Chocolate Nut Berry Cups	187
Chicken Alfredo Pasta Bowl	190
Jalapeno Cheddar Appetizers	193
Mini Apple Pies	196

Foreword:

These are the recipes of all three of my muffin tin recipe books – Muffin Tin Meals, Muffin Tin Madness and Muffin Tin Cuisine. Whether you are a newcomer to cooking meals in muffin tins or just want to thumb through a bigger collection of recipes, I hope that this collection will bring many satisfying meals and treats your way.

I put these recipes together when I realized that I was overeating, putting my family at risk with nonstick pans and wasting precious time washing dishes. Muffin tin recipes were the perfect solution for all of my problems! I only make what we need, spend much less time with the dishes and more with my family.

Book One: Muffin Tin Menus

Breakfast Muffins

These aren't really muffins, but you will need a muffin or cupcake tin. You can pop them right out and eat them one-handed. I do not supply measurements because the recipe is really about 'eyeballing' it.

Ingredients:

- Bread

- Butter

- Eggs

- Ham

- Heavy Cream

- Optional: Cheese, Salt, and Pepper

Cookware:

Muffin/Cupcake Tin

Directions:

1. Preheat oven to 350 degrees Fahrenheit (176 degrees Celsius).

2. Butter the bread on one side and press it into the muffin tin, butter side up. Insert into the oven for about 10 minutes. Do NOT remove the toasted bread from the tin.

3. Place a piece of ham (any meat product you like should work) on the bottom of the toasted bread cups.

4. Crack an egg over the ham, being careful to keep it neat.

5. Spoon a little bit of cream over the top of the egg. The cream will ensure that the egg will cook evenly on top.

6. Season however you would like. Depending on your oven, it may take between 10 and 20 minutes for the eggs to properly cook. They will be done once the egg whites become opaque.

7. Pop them out and eat; no silverware or plates required.

Lasagna Bites – Version 1

This only requires a cupcake tin and has all of the ingredients that give lasagna that special taste. The one thing it is missing is the pasta, but it more than makes up for it by being easy to make and easy to cleanup.

Ingredients:

- Pre-Made Biscuit Dough

- Cooked Ground Beef (or veggies, if you prefer)

- Ricotta Cheese

- Shredded Cheese (mozzarella or cheddar is fine)

- Tomato Paste

- Sweet Tomato Sauce

- Eggs

Cookware:

Muffin/Cupcake Tin, Mixing Bowl

Directions:

1. Preheat oven to 375 degrees Fahrenheit (190 Celsius).

2. Roll out biscuits enough to flatten them. Stretch and place into muffin pans to form dough cups.

3. Add cooked ground beef or vegetables and sauce mixture.

4. In a mixing bowl, combine ricotta cheese and egg (this makes the ricotta easier to spread).

5. Spread a bit of ricotta on top.

6. Sprinkle with shredded cheese.

7. Brown in oven until the edges of the dough turns golden. Oven times will vary, but it should be between 15 - 30 minutes.

8. Enjoy!

Lasagna Bites – Version 2

This is a different take on lasagna cups that also tastes great. They look a little more elegant served on a plate than the first version because of the wonton wrappers. These can be found in the frozen vegetable aisle of most supermarkets.

Ingredients:

- 1/2 Lb. (455 G) Cooked Ground Beef

- 1/2 Lb. (455 G) Cooked Italian Sausage

- 24 Wonton Wrappers

- 2 cups Shredded Parmesan Cheese

- 2 cups Shredded Mozzarella Cheese

- 1 cup Ricotta Cheese

- 2 cups Pasta Sauce

- Basil Leaves

Cookware:

Muffin/Cupcake Tin,

Directions:

1. Preheat oven to 375 degrees Fahrenheit (190 Celsius).

2. Grease muffin/cupcake tin

3. Press a wonton wrapper into each up. It is OK for the corners to come out. They will make it easy to pull out the finished product later.

4. Layer the ingredients. Parmesan Cheese – Basil Leaf – Mozzarella Cheese – Meat – Ricotta Cheese – Pasta Sauce – Parmesan Cheese.

5. Bake until the edges of the wonton wrappers turn golden brown, about 15-20 minutes.

6. Remove from the oven and allow to cool for 5 minutes.

7. Use a knife to help ease out the cups.

Parmesan Spinach Bites

These healthy side items are a good way to sneak in good-tasting veggies. Measurements for this recipe will create 8 servings.

Ingredients:

- 12 Oz. Baby Spinach

- 1/2 Cup Ricotta or Cottage Cheese

- 1/2 Cup Finely Shredded Parmesan

- 2 Large Eggs

- 1 Clove Minced Garlic

- Pinch of Salt

- Pinch of Pepper

Cookware:

Muffin/Cupcake Tin, Food Processor, Mixing Bowl

Directions:

1. Preheat oven to 400 degrees Fahrenheit (200 Celsius).

2. Finely chop the spinach leaves in the processor or with a fine knife.

3. Add salt, pepper, eggs, garlic, parmesan and stir.

4. Coat the muffin/cupcake tin with nonstick spray or use liners. Fill them with the spinach mixture.

5. Bake for 20 minutes. They will not look cooked around the center when you first remove them from the oven. Allow them to sit for 5 minutes and they will be completely cooked.

6. Sprinkle with parmesan cheese and serve warm.

Stuffed Chicken Breast

This dish creates perfect portions and allows for a lot of imagination. Feel free to get creative with the stuffing.

Ingredients:

- Boneless Chicken Breasts

- Bacon (microwaveable to save time)

- Cheese Slices (cheddar, Swiss, etc.)

- Bread Crumbs

- Egg

Cookware:

Muffin/Cupcake Tin, 2 Small Bowls

Directions:

1. Preheat oven to 375 degrees Fahrenheit (190 Celsius).

2. Filet the chicken breasts in half and pound them to tenderize the meat.

3. Microwave the bacon (or cook in a frying pan, if you do not mind needing to wash more dishes).

4. Place a slice of cheese and a piece of bacon on the center of each chicken breast you are preparing.

5. Prepare an egg wash in a bowl by combining an egg with water or milk.

6. Pinch the ends of the chicken breast together, forming a ball. Dip this into the egg white and then the breadcrumbs.

7. Press each stuffed chicken breast, pinched side down, into the muffin/cupcake tin. Cook for 40 minutes.

Chicken Taco Cups

These take under 20 minutes and are fun to eat. You can use leftover chicken, prepackaged chicken or make some up fresh. Ground meats and poultry would work as well.

Ingredients:

- Flour Tortillas

- Cooked Chicken

- Shredded Lettuce

- Salsa

- Shredded Cheese

Cookware:

Muffin/Cupcake Tin, 4" (approx. 10cm) Round Cookie Cutter (or scissors)

Directions:

1. Preheat 350 degrees Fahrenheit (175 degrees Celsius) and grease the muffin/cupcake tin.

2. Microwave the tortillas in a microwavable-safe plate for 15 seconds.

3. Use the cookie cutter to trim each tortilla or trim them down to a circle with a 4" (approx. 10 cm) diameter.

4. Press the tortillas into the muffin/cupcake tin with your hands or the bottom of a glass cup.

5. Spoon some of your chicken filling into the taco shell.

6. Layer on the lettuce, salsa and cheese.

7. Place the muffin/cupcake tin in the preheated oven for 10 to 15 minutes, until the cheese is melty.

8. Allow them to cool until you can pop them out without burning your fingers.

Mini Meatloaves

These little bites of soul food are easy to make ahead of time. They are great for bagged lunches and make portion control a cinch.

Ingredients:

- 1-1/2 Lbs. (680 G) Ground Beef, Raw

- 2 Eggs

- 1 Cup Onion, Chopped

- 1 Cup Crackers, Crushed

- 2 Garlic Cloves, Minced

- 1 Tsp. Worcestershire Sauce

- 1 Tsp. Oregano

- 1 Cup Ketchup (Or Tomato-Base BBQ Sauce)

Cookware:

Muffin/cupcake tin, saucepan

Directions:

1. Preheat oven to 350 degrees Fahrenheit (176 degrees Celsius).

2. Grease the muffin/cupcake tin.

3. Sautee the onion, garlic and oregano over medium-high heat. Remove from the stove eye.

4. Except for half of the ketchup, mix everything together. Do not cook the ground beef, it will bake in the oven.

5. Spread the mixture evenly in 12 muffin/cupcake cups.

6. Spoon remaining ketchup on top of each mini meatloaf.

7. Bake for about 25 minutes, when internal temperature reaches 160 degrees Fahrenheit (71 Celsius).

8. Enjoy!

Muffin Cup Corn Dogs

These corndogs cook up quickly and are fun to eat. You can use them for parties, snacks or even a meal. Children and their teachers love these so much more than chips for parties because there is never any arguing about who got more than who, and there are no dangerous sticks for them to play 'swordfight' with! These carnival treats are so easy to make that they are sure to become a staple in your cooking rotation.

Ingredients:

- Jiffy Cornbread Mix

- Hotdogs

Cookware:

Muffin/Cupcake Tin, Mixing Bowl

Directions:

1. Preheat 350 degrees Fahrenheit (175 degrees Celsius).

2. Grease the tin. Prepare Jiffy cornbread batter according to package directions.

3. Cut hot dogs into pieces that are just long enough to peek out of the muffin/cupcake tin.

4. Fill the tin cups about 2/3 of the way.

5. Stick the hotdog in the center and bake until cake appears golden brown.

6. Remove the tin from the oven and allow the food to sit for a minute.

Handheld Hash Brown Casseroles

These are not messy to make and are the perfect breakfast comfort food. They reheat well in a microwave when wrapped with a paper towel. They are also an attractive addition to any special brunch. These measurements can make 24 servings, but feel free to cut it down accordingly for fewer casseroles.

Ingredients:

- 1 Pound (455 G) Sausage – Cooked And Crumbled
- 1 (20 Ounce) Package Frozen Hash Browns

- 4 Eggs

- 1/2 Cup Milk

- 3 Tablespoons Melted Butter

- 1 Cup Cubed Ham

- 1/2 Teaspoon Black Pepper

- 1/2 Cup Diced Bell Peppers

- 1 Cup Shredded Cheddar Cheese

Cookware:

Muffin/Cupcake Tin, Mixing Bowl, Frying Pan

Directions:

1. Preheat 350 degrees Fahrenheit (175 degrees Celsius).

2. Grease muffin/cupcake tin.

3. Whisk eggs and milk.

4. Add all other ingredients and mix until they are close to being evenly distributed.

5. Fill cups 2/3 of the way.

6. Bake until center passes the clean toothpick test, about 25-30 minutes.

7. When done, remove carefully with a knife.

Apple Crisp Cups

with REAL Apples

Who wouldn't love a warm apple crisp straight from the oven? These are affordable versions of the treat that come in perfect portions and go great with ice cream! These measurements are for 12 servings.

Ingredients:

- 3/4 Large McIntosh Apples - Peeled, Cored, And Chopped

- 1 Tbsp. Water

- 1-1/2 Teaspoons White Sugar

- 1/8 Teaspoon Ground Cinnamon (To Taste)

- 1/2 Cup All-Purpose Flour

- 1/2 Cup Rolled Oats

- 1/4 Cup And 2 Tbsp. Brown Sugar

- 1/4 Tsp. Ground Cinnamon

- 1/8 Tsp. Ground Nutmeg

- 1/4 Cup And 2 Tbsp. Butter

Cookware:

Muffin/Cupcake Tin, Saucepan, Mixing Bowl

Directions:

1. Preheat oven to 350 degrees F (175 degrees C).

2. Grease muffin/cupcake tins

3. Mix apples, water, sugar, and 1/2 tsp. of cinnamon in saucepan over medium-low heat for 5 minutes.

4. Mix the remaining dry ingredients in a mixing bowl.

5. Combine dry mix with softened butter until the mixture takes on a crumb-like consistency.

6. Use the mixture to create crusts for the apple mixture. Do this by pressing it against the bottom and sides with the back of a spoon. You may have some leftover crust.

7. Pour the apple mixture into each cup, filling it about 2/3 of the way.

8. Bake until golden brown, about 15-20 minutes.

Mini Quiche

This fancy-sounding egg pie is actually a down-to-earth and hardy meal. It packs a lot of protein and has plenty of great flavors. These measurements are for 12 servings.

Ingredients:

- 12 Slices Bread

- 1 Onion, Grated

- 1/2 Cup Shredded Swiss Cheese

- 1 Cup Milk

- 4 Eggs

- 1 Teaspoon Dry Mustard

- 1 Pinch Black Pepper

Cookware:

Muffin/Cupcake Tin, Mixing Bowl, Knife

Directions:

1. Preheat oven to 375 degrees F (190 degrees C)

2. Grease muffin/cupcake tins

3. Trim the slices of bread into circles with a knife.

4. Press a slice of bread into each tin opening.

5. Evenly disperse onion and shredded cheese in each tin opening.

6. Mix remaining ingredients in a mixing bowl.

7. Pour into egg mixture into tin openings, about 2/3 full.

8. Bake until a toothpick comes out clean from the center, about 20 minutes.

Portion-Perfect Frittatas

Frittatas are great anytime of the day. This recipe is so healthy that you may want to go all-out and switch the eggs out for an egg substitute to keep it cholesterol free. Salsa, sour cream and tortilla chips on the side make this a tasty party treat. Measurements are for 12.

Ingredients:

- 6 Oz. (170 g) Frozen Chopped Spinach, Thawed And Drained

- 1 Cup Ricotta Cheese

- 2 Tbsps. Sour Cream

- 1/2 Cup Grated Parmesan Cheese

- 1/2 Cup Shredded Cheddar Cheese

- 4 Eggs

- 1/4 Cup Milk

- 1 Tsp. Ground Cumin

- 1/4 Tsp. Ground Black Pepper

- 1/2 Tsp. Lemon Pepper

- 2 Tbsps. Dried Parsley

- 3 Tbsps. Salsa

Cookware:

Muffin/Cupcake Tin, Medium and Small Mixing Bowls

Directions:

1. Preheat oven to oven to 375 degrees F (190 degrees C).

2. Grease muffin/cupcake tin.

3. In medium mixing bowl, combine spinach and all three cheeses.

4. In small mixing bowl, beat the eggs and the remaining ingredients.

5. Pour the contents of the egg mixture into the medium mixing bowl and stir together.

6. Pour the frittata mixture into the muffin/cupcake tin, filling each cup about 2/3 full.

7. Bake for 20-25 minutes.

8. Remove from oven and allow frittatas to cool for 5 minutes before eating.

Asian Dumplings

You can pair these with your favorite sauce for an exotic lunch or romantic dinner. These will be larger than what you will find at an Asian restaurant and will be much more filling. These measurements will serve 6.

Ingredients:

- 1 Pound Cooked Ground Turkey (or Beef)
- 2 Chopped Green Onions
- 1 Tsp. Grated Fresh Ginger
- 1 Pinch Black Pepper

- 1 Tbsp. Soy Sauce

- 1 Grated Garlic Clove

- 24 Wonton Wrappers

- Cooking Spray

Cookware:

Muffin/Cupcake Tin, Mixing Bowl, Brush

Directions:

1. Preheat oven to 400 degrees Fahrenheit (205 Celsius).

2. Grease muffin/cupcake tin

3. Mix all of the ingredients (except the wonton wrappers) well in a mixing bowl.

4. Brush one side of the wonton wrapper with water (not too much – you do not want it to be soggy).

5. Gently press the wonton wrapper into **EVERY OTHER** opening.

6. Fill each one with 1 tbsp. of the meat mixture.

7. Fold the ends of the wonton wrapper. It is almost like wrapping a little food present. Lightly brush the edges with water to help it seal.

8. Fill the empty muffin/cupcake tin cups halfway with water. The water will steam the

dumplings, which is a **required** step in the cooking process.

9. Cover tin with aluminum foil.

10. Bake for 10 minutes.

11. Remove foil.

12. Spray dumplings with cooking spray.

13. Turn on the broiler and pull out the tin after 2 minutes.

14. Enjoy with your favorite dipping sauce!

Mini Pizzas

These reheat well and cook up in less than half an hour. You can find pizza dough in the refrigerated section by prepared cookie dough. Some supermarkets also make their own and sell it in-house.

Ingredients:

- Pizza Dough

- Pizza Sauce, 1 Tbsp. per Mini Pizza

- 1 Cup Toppings per 6 Mini Pizzas

- Shredded Cheese, 1 Tbsp. per Mini Pizza

Cookware:

Muffin/Cupcake Tin

Directions:

1. Preheat oven to 400 degrees Fahrenheit (205 Celsius).

2. Separate the pizza dough into golf ball sizes sections.

3. Roll out each ball into a flat, 5" (13 cm) circle.

4. Grease the muffin/cupcake tin.

5. Press the dough circles into the muffin/cupcake tin openings. It does not have to be perfect.

6. Spoon in pizza sauce.

7. Place 1/6 Cup of toppings in each mini pizza.

8. Top with cheese.

9. Bake until the top edges are golden brown, about 15-20 minutes.

10. Enjoy!

Frozen Fruit Treats

Forget the oven. These sweet treats are healthy, only use two ingredients and are made in the freezer. Kids often nickname these 'frozen cupcakes.'

Ingredients:

- Bananas

- Yogurt, Any Flavor

Cookware:

Muffin/Cupcake Tin

Directions:

1. Cut the banana up into small pieces.

2. Put banana chunks into each tin opening. How many is up to taste.

3. Fill each tin opening with yogurt. Make sure that the banana pieces are all coated.

4. Freeze for 2-3 hours.

5. Enjoy!

Two-Bite French Toast

These are a lot less messy to make than normal French toast, and you do not even have to heat up the non-stick pan. Use muffin/cupcake liners to cut cleanup time even more. These measurements will make 4 portion-perfect French toasts. Get as creative as you want with the syrup and bread.

Ingredients:

- 6 Eggs

- 1.5 Cups Heavy Cream (Half And Half Is Fine)

- 4 Cups Cubed Bread (Try Texas Toast)

- 2 Tbsps. Sugar

- 2 Tbsps. Melted Butter

- 2 Tsps. Vanilla

- 1 Pinch Cinnamon

- 1 Pinch Salt

- 6 Tbsps. Pancake Syrup

Cookware:

Muffin/Cupcake Tin, Two Mixing Bowls

Directions:

1. Put the butter and bread aside; whisk all other ingredients together in a mixing bowl.

2. In a separate mixing bowl, coat the cubed bread with the melted butter.

3. Lightly press the buttery bread cubes into the muffin/cupcake tin openings.

4. Evenly pour the egg and cream mixture over the bread.

5. Preheat 350 degrees Fahrenheit (175 degrees Celsius). Wait until this point to preheat the oven. It will give the bread a chance to soak up all of the ingredients and flavors.

6. Once the oven is preheated, sprinkle sugar on top and bake for 20 minutes.

7. Remove from oven and allow to rest for 5 minutes before serving.

Handheld Bacon and Eggs

No collection of recipes is complete without at least one bacon entry. I would eat these any time of the day, but they make an impressive breakfast food. You can make a few extra and keep them around for later. These measurements will make approximately 12 portions. Most people will eat two of them.

Ingredients:

- 9 Eggs

- 1/2 Lb. (225 G) Bacon, Cooked And Chopped

- 1 Tomato, Diced

- 2 Green Onions, Sliced

- 1 Cup Mushrooms, Diced

- 1 Cup Greens (Arugula, Spinach, Etc.), Chopped

- 1 Sprig (Or 2 Tbsps.) Thyme

Cookware:

Muffin/Cupcake Tin, Mixing Bowl

Directions:

1. Preheat oven to oven to 375 degrees F (190 degrees C).

2. Grease muffin/cupcake tin.

3. In a mixing bowl, beat all of the ingredients together.

4. Evenly distribute mixture among 12 muffin/cupcake cup openings.

5. Bake until the centers are set, about 20 minutes.

6. Remove from oven and allow to cool for 5 minutes before eating.

7. Enjoy!

Mini Chicken Pot Pie

These are better than any premium pot pie that you can get premade in the freezer section. These mini versions are much easier to make than the traditional pot pie recipes. These measurements will make 8.

Ingredients:

- 1 Canister Premade Biscuits (You Get What You Pay For Here)

- 1 Can (19 Oz.) Chicken Noodle Soup, Drained of Broth

- 2 tbsps. Butter

- 1 tsp. Italian Seasoning

- 1/4 Cup Shredded Mozzarella Cheese

- 1 Pinch Garlic Powder

Cookware:

Muffin/Cupcake Tin

Directions:

1. Preheat oven to oven to 375 degrees F (190 degrees C).

2. Grease muffin/cupcake pan.

3. Split biscuit dough into 8 biscuits. Divide each of these in half.

4. Press a biscuit halve into each muffin/cupcake cup opening, making sure to press up the side walls.

5. Spoon the drained soup into the cups.

6. Seal the tops of the cups with the other biscuit halves.

7. Brush butter on the tops.

8. Sprinkle Italian seasoning and garlic powder on butter.

9. Sprinkle cheese on top of seasonings.

10. Bake until edges are golden brown, about 14-17 minutes.

11. Remove carefully with a sharp knife.

12. Enjoy!

Book Two: Muffin Tin Madness

Morning Sunrise Muffins

These oven-poached eggs sit on a maple-flavored piece of toast and pieces of bacon. The subtle sweet flavor really compliments the savory bacon and poached egg. Measurements given will create 6 muffin cups.

Ingredients:

- 6 Large Eggs

- 6 Slices Bacon, Cooked and Chopped into Bits

- 6 Slices Bread (White Or Wheat)

- 1/4 Cup Butter, Melted

- 6 Tbsps. Heavy Cream

- 1-1/2 Tbsps. Butter, Melted

- 1-1/2 Tsps. Maple Syrup

- Optional: Salt and Black Pepper to Taste

- Optional: 6 Tbsps. Shredded Cheddar Cheese

Cookware:

Muffin/Cupcake Tin, Small Mixing Bowl

Directions:

1. Preheat oven to 375 degrees Fahrenheit (190 Celsius).

2. Grease muffin tins.

3. Flatten the bread as thin as possible with a rolling pin (or the side of a soup can).

4. Combine maple syrup and butter in a small mixing bowl.

5. Press each slice of bread into a muffin cup, then brush the inside of each one with the butter and syrup.

6. Bake until crispy, 3-5 minutes. Remove from oven.

7. Sprinkle bits of bacon into muffin cups.

8. Crack an egg into each muffin cup. Top each with 1 Tbsp. cream (this is necessary for the cooking process).

9. Season with salt and pepper to taste. Top with shredded cheese.

10. Bake until egg whites are cooked, about 10-15 minutes.

Homemade Breakfast Sandwiches

You can go to a fast food restaurant and wonder what exactly is in your breakfast sandwich, or you can make these beauties up in minutes and freeze the extras for another day. Add any condiments you want and consider trying different cheeses. Measurements supplies will yield 6 sandwiches.

Ingredients:

- 6 English Muffins

- 6 Large eggs

- Optional: 6 Slices of Cheese (any kind you like)

- Optional: Ham

Cookware:

Muffin/Cupcake Tin

Directions:

1. Preheat oven to 350 degrees Fahrenheit (175 Celsius).

2. Grease the muffin tins.

3. Crack 1 egg in each muffin tin cup.

4. Bake for 10-15 minutes, to desired 'doneness.' The less time they are baked, the runnier they are.

5. While waiting on the eggs, slice your English muffins in half lengthwise.

6. Optional: Place a slice of cheese and ham on top halves of sandwiches.

7. When eggs are ready, they should easily slide out with a little prodding from a knife.

8. Place one egg in each sandwich.

9. Serve immediately or freeze for later.

10. If making this ahead of time and freezing, make sure to wrap the sandwiches in a paper towel when microwaving.

Dreamy Pineapple Coconut Pies

Coconut and pineapple go together like peanut butter and jelly. These delightful mini pies are light and tropical enough to make anyone feel like they have been touched by a little bit of Caribbean magic. Yields 20 mini pies.

Ingredients:

Filling

- 8 Oz. (226.5 g) Pineapple, Crushed
- 1 Tbsp. Honey
- 1 Tbsp. Cornstarch

Dough

- 1.76 Oz. (50 g) Almonds

- 6 Tbsps. Confectioners' Sugar

- 1/2 Cup Whole-Wheat Pastry Flour

- 1/4 Cup All-Purpose Flour

- 1/4 Cup Unsalted Cold Butter

- 3 Tbsps. Olive Oil

- 2 Tbsps. Shredded Coconut, Unsweetened

- 1 Tbsp. Cornstarch

- 1 Dash Salt

- 1 Dash Vanilla Extract

Cookware:

Muffin/Cupcake Tin, Cupcake Liners, Saucepan, Food Processor

Directions:

For filling

1. Over medium heat, combine pineapple, cornstarch and honey in a small saucepan. Stir frequently until thickened, about 3 minutes.

2. Take thickened filling mixture off of the heat and allow it to cool while you work on the dough.

For dough

1. Grind almonds in a food processor.

2. Add sugar to food processor, combine.

3. Add both flours, combine.

4. Add butter and combine, one tablespoon at a time.

5. Add oil and process mixture.

6. Add remaining ingredients (not the pie filling) to food processor and combine until mixture is a little crumbly.

All together

1. Preheat oven to 350 degrees Fahrenheit (175 Celsius).

2. Place 1 tablespoon of dough into each muffin cup. You should have 1/2 cup leftover.

3. Press the dough outwards and up the sides.

4. Spoon 1-2 Tsps. filling in each cup.

5. Sprinkle crumbs from the leftover crust on top of each mini pie.

6. Bake until golden, about 20-25 minutes.

Portion-Perfect Crab Cakes

Crab cakes are delicious enough by themselves, but you can take this up to the next level and put them in a hoagie roll with coleslaw or a unique boardwalk sandwich. Makes 12 crab cakes.

Ingredients:

- 1 lb. (454 kg) crabmeat

- 2 Cups Breadcrumbs

- 3 Scallions, Sliced

- 3 Large Eggs

- 1/2 Bell Pepper, Minced (any type)

- 1/4 Cup Mayonnaise

- 1 Tsp. Hot Sauce

- 1 Dash Celery Salt

- 1 Pinch Ground Black Pepper

- Optional: Lemon Wedges for Garnish

Cookware:

Muffin/Cupcake Tin, Large Mixing Bowl

Directions:

1. Preheat oven to 450 degrees Fahrenheit (232 Celsius).

2. Grease muffin/cupcake tin.

3. Mix all ingredients together in a large mixing bowl.

4. Distribute mixture evenly among 12 muffin cups.

5. Bake until crispy, about 20-25 minutes.

6. Garnish with lemon wedges if desired.

7. Serve warm.

Sinfully Simple Chocolate Lava Cupcakes

This is so much easier to make than I thought was possible. All you need to really do is freeze the chocolate lava to make sure it melts at the right speed during the baking process. Makes 24 magnificent mini lava cakes.

Ingredients:

- 1 Box Chocolate Cake Mix

- 1 Bag Chocolate Chips (Any Type You Like)

- 2 Tbsps. Butter, Melted

- 1 Tbsp. Light Corn Syrup

Cookware:

Muffin/Cupcake Tin, Medium Mixing Bowl, Microwaveable-Safe Bowl

Directions:

1. Create the lava filling a half hour ahead of time. In a microwave-safe bowl, melt the chocolate by microwaving on high and stirring at 20 second intervals.

2. Add butter and corn syrup to melted chocolate, stir well.

3. Place chocolate mixture in the freezer, covered to protect from freezer burn.

7. Once the chocolate is frozen, preheat oven to 350 degrees Fahrenheit (175 Celsius).

4. Grease muffin/cupcake tin or use paper liners.

5. Prepare chocolate cake mix according to box instructions.

6. Fill 24 muffin cups about 1/3 of the way full with batter.

7. Remove frozen chocolate mixture from freezer and chop into 24 pieces.

8. Place a chunk of frozen chocolate into each cup.

9. Pour remaining batter on top, each cup should be about 2/3 full.

10. Bake until cake is cooked, about 20-25 minutes.

11. Peel of liner (if used) and serve upside down!

Gourmet Lava Cakes with Mocha Sauce

These are sure to be a hit. The notes of mocha are not overpowering, but they definitely set the scene for this lava cake. Make sure to plan ahead when making this recipe. The flavor is too unique to be found in a premade mix.

Ingredients:

- 4 Oz. Bittersweet Chocolate, Chopped

- 2 Tbsps. Unsalted Butter, Sliced Into Pieces

- 1 Tbsp. White Granulated Sugar

- 1-1/2 Tbsps. Heavy Cream

- 2 Tsps. Instant Espresso

- 1 Tbsp. Light Corn Syrup

- 1 Large Egg

- 2 Tbsps. Canola Oil

- 1 Tsp. Vanilla Extract

- 1 Dash Salt

- 5 Tbsps. Confectioners' Sugar

- 3 Tbsps. Flour, All Purpose

- 1 Tbsp. Dutch-Process Cocoa Powder

- 1-3 Teaspoons Hot Water

Cookware:

Muffin/Cupcake Tin, 2 Microwave-Safe Bowls, Medium Mixing Bowl, Whisk

Directions:

Chocolate Filling

1. Grease muffin/cupcake tin.

2. In a microwave-safe bowl, microwave chocolate and butter for one minute on the high setting.

3. Stir butter and chocolate, then continue to microwave and stir for 20 second intervals until completely melted.

4. In a separate microwave-safe bowl, mix together sugar, cream and half of the instant

espresso. Microwave for 20 seconds. Stir until sugar granules are completely melted.

5. Add half of the melted chocolate mixture into the second bowl (the one with the espresso, cream and sugar mixture).

6. Add corn syrup and stir until mixture is smooth.

7. Cover and freeze for 30 minutes.

Batter

1. Preheat oven to 350 degrees Fahrenheit (175 Celsius).

2. In a medium mixing bowl, whisk together egg, vanilla, oil, vanilla and leftover espresso mix until smooth.

3. Reheat the remaining chocolate and butter mixture in the microwave, stirring at 20 second intervals until warm.

4. Pour half of the chocolate mixture into the egg mixture. Whisk until well blended.

5. Add second half of chocolate mixture. Whisk until well blended.

6. Mix flour, cocoa and confectioner's sugar into the batter.

Assembling

1. Take filling out of freezer.

2. Place 1 Tsp. in each muffin cup. Half of the batter should remain after this step.

3. Place 1/2 Tsp. frozen filling in each center. Remainder will be used for sauce.

4. Distribute remaining batter across muffin cups, covering the filling.

5. Bake until edges are dry, but centers still look underdone, about 7-10 minutes.

6. Cool on a wire rack.

7. If cakes stick to muffin/cupcake tin, loosen with a knife.

8. Add hot water to remaining filling and stir to create chocolate sauce.

9. Serve molten lava cupcakes upside down with chocolate sauce drizzled on top.

Mini Greek Pizzas

I find that these small pizzas are good for portion control. One muffin-sized portion is about equal to one traditional slice, so keep that in mind! You will be making real dough in this recipe, but you can skip out on that section if you buy premade dough. Yields about 6 servings.

Ingredients:

- 2 Tbsps. Extra-Virgin Olive Oil

- 1 Large Egg, Beaten

- 2/3 Cup Onion, Finely Chopped

- 2/3 Cup Red Bell Pepper, Finely Chopped

- 1/3 Cup Pastry Flour

- 1/3 Cup Flour, All-Purpose

- 1/3 Cup Milk, Part-Skim

- 1/3 Cup Feta Cheese, Crumbled

- 2 Tbsps. Kalamata Olives, Chopped

- 2 Tsps. Baking Powder

- 1 Tsp. Sugar

- 1 Dash Garlic Powder

- 1 Dash Teaspoon Salt

- 2 Tbsps. Tomato Paste

- 1 Pinch Oregano

Cookware:

Muffin/Cupcake Tin, Large Skillet, Large Mixing Bowl, Medium Mixing Bowl

Directions:

1. Heat olive oil over medium heat in large skillet.

2. Add bell pepper and onion, stirring for 5 minutes, until onion is tender.

3. Transfer to large bowl and allow vegetables to cool.

4. Preheat oven to 400 degrees Fahrenheit (200 Celsius).

5. Grease muffin/cupcake tin.

6. Whisk flours, baking powder, sugar, garlic powder, oregano, salt in medium bowl.

7. Place milk, feta cheese, egg, olives and tomato paste into large mixing bowl with onion mixture and stir together.

8. Make a deep indentation (or well) in the dry ingredients and slowly pour the wet mixture in.

9. Combine until well mixed.

10. Fill muffin cups 2/3 of the way.

11. Bake until slightly brown, about 15 minutes.

12. Cool for 5 minutes before serving.

Monkey Bread

Cinnamon sweet and easy to eat, every age group can appreciate a warm handful of monkey bread. I like to keep cream cheese icing on hand as dip for the pieces of bread that I break off. Consider it a deconstructed cinnamon roll. Measurements given will yield 12.

Ingredients:

- 1 Can Premade Biscuits/Crescent

- 6 Tbsps. Sugar

- 3 Tbsps. Cinnamon

- 1/2 Cup Butter

- 1/2 Cup Light Brown Sugar

Cookware:

Muffin/Cupcake Tin, Scissors, Large Mixing Bowl, Cupcake Liners (if desired), Microwavable Bowl

Directions:

1. Preheat oven to 350 degrees Fahrenheit (175 Celsius).

2. Grease muffin/cupcake tin or place paper liners in muffin cups.

3. Cut each biscuit/crescent roll into pieces, about 5 or 6.

4. In a large mixing bowl, combine cinnamon and sugar.

5. Toss dough pieces in the cinnamon-sugar mixture.

6. Distribute the dough pieces among the 12 muffin cups as evenly as possible.

7. Sprinkle any remaining sugar-cinnamon mixture over dough.

8. In a microwaveable bowl, place butter and brown sugar. Microwave until butter is melted.

9. Stir and pour evenly over dough.

10. Bake according to directions on the dough package, until edges appear golden brown.

11. Allow monkey bread to cool slightly before serving.

Cranberry Brie Puffs

There is something about the tart and creamy taste of these that is addictive. The natural salt of the cheese accents the cranberry's sweetness very well. You will run out of these faster than you think. Measurements provided will yield 20.

Ingredients:

- 1 Cup Cranberry Sauce

- 1 Triangle Brie

- Puff Pastry Sheet

Directions:

1. Preheat oven to 375 degrees Fahrenheit (190 Celsius).

2. Cut pastry puff sheet into 3 inch (about 8 cm) squares.

3. Press each square into the muffin cups.

4. Place a 1 inch (2.5 cm) square of brie in the middle of each muffin cup.

5. Top with 1 Tbsp. cranberry sauce.

6. Bake until pastry corners are light brown, about 10 minutes.

7. Allow to cool about 5 minutes.

8. Serve warm.

Mushroom Brie Tarts

This is indulgent grownup food, although some sophisticated kids may like it. Brie has been a favorite of party planners for years. You can make these for yourself whenever you would like. Measurements will yield 24.

Ingredients:

- 1 Can Crescent Rolls

- 6 Oz. Portabella Mushrooms, Finely Chopped

- 3 Oz Brie Cheese

- 4 Green Onions, Sliced

- 2 Tbsps. Butter Margarine

- 2 Cloves Garlic, Finely Chopped

- 1 Tsp. Mustard (Dijon or Brown)

Cookware:

Mini Muffin/Cupcake Tin, Small Skillet

Directions:

1. Preheat oven to 375 degrees Fahrenheit (190 Celsius).

2. Grease mini muffin/cupcake tin.

3. In small skillet, heat mushrooms, garlic and butter over medium heat until mushrooms have absorbed butter.

4. Add onions and mustard.

5. Unroll dough and separate into 4 rectangles each.

6. Press each rectangle of dough into a muffin cup.

7. Spoon 1 Tbsp. mushroom mixture in each dough.

8. Bake until golden brown, 10-12 minutes.

9. Cut brie into 24 pieces and place 1 in each muffin cup.

10. Take muffin tin out of oven and place 1 piece of brie in each muffin cup.

11. Return tin to oven and bake an additional 3 minutes, until cheese is soft.

12. Cool before serving.

Cheddar Sausage Biscuits

Filling side dishes like these are great for fast lunches or finger foods. I think they are marvelous for picnics when the weather warms up. Try them with soup when it is still warm outside and add your favorite spices, if you want an extra kick. Measurements provided yield 16 servings.

Ingredients:

- 5 Italian Sausages

- 1-1/2 Cups Cheddar Cheese, Grated

- 1 Can Premade Biscuits

- 1 McIntosh Apple, Chopped

- 1/2 Onion, Chopped (About 1 Cup)

- 12 Pinches Rosemary

Cookware:

Muffin/Cupcake Tin

Directions:

1. Pull the casing off of the sausages and crumble with a fork.

2. Put crumbled sausage in a large skillet and bring up to a medium heat.

3. Add chopped onion and apple after two or three minutes.

4. Continue to cook until sausage is cooked throughout.

5. Preheat oven to 350 degrees Fahrenheit (177 Celsius).

6. Grease muffin/cupcake tin.

7. Pull 6 biscuits in half, lengthwise. The remaining 2 biscuits (if you purchase a can of 8) will not be used in this recipe.

8. Press the biscuit halves into the muffin cups. Make sure to press the dough up the sides.

9. Evenly distribute cheese into each muffin cup.

10. Fill each muffin cup with the sausage mixture.

11. Top each one with a pinch of rosemary.

12. Bake until edges of biscuits are golden brown, about 15 minutes.

13. Serve warm and refrigerate leftovers.

Spinach and Feta Bites

Sophisticated and portion-perfect for parties, this finger food is filling and does not look amateur. Measurements yield 12 bites.

Ingredients:

- 1 Lb. (454 G) Spinach

- 8 Oz. Feta Cheese, Crumbled

- 1 Large Egg, Beaten

- 1 Clove Garlic, Minced

- 1/4 Onion, Finely Chopped

- 2 Tbsp. Parsley, Chopped

- Salt And Pepper

- 2 Sheets Puff Pastry

- 1/4 Cup and 2 Tbsps. Butter

Cookware:

Muffin/Cupcake Tin, Medium Saucepan, Colander, Large Mixing Bowl, Microwave-Safe Bowl

Directions:

1. Preheat oven to 375 degrees Fahrenheit (190 Celsius).

2. Spray saucepan with cooking spray. On medium-high heat, cook garlic and onion until onion is translucent.

3. Add spinach a little bit at a time.

4. Stir and cook until spinach appears wilted throughout.

5. Pour the food in the saucepan into a colander and drain excess liquid.

6. If spinach is still damp, pat dry with a towel.

7. In a large mixing bowl, combine spinach mixture, beaten egg, feta and parsley.

8. Melt 1/4 cup butter in microwave-safe bowl. Make sure that it does not 'boil.'

7. Brush pastry sheets with butter.

8. Spread spinach mixture on both pastry sheets, leaving 1/2 inch (1.27 cm) edges clean.

9. Roll up pastry into as tight a roll as possible.

10. Slice into 12 segments.

11. Grease the muffin/cupcake tin.

12. Place the spirals into muffin cups.

13. Brush remaining butter lightly over the spirals.

14. Bake for 20 minutes.

15. Serve warm and refrigerate leftovers.

Mini Pineapple Upside-Down Cakes

These should be a good break from the mundane dessert. They pack a lot of natural sweetness and uniquely bold fruit flavors. This dessert was popular in the '50s and deserves a comeback. Measurements yield 12 individual cakes.

Ingredients:

- 1 Box White or Yellow Cake Mix

- 1 14-Oz. Can Pineapple Pieces

- 3/4 cup brown sugar

- 3/4 a stick of butter

Cookware

Muffin/Cupcake Tin, Microwaveable Bowl

Directions:

1. Preheat oven to 400 degrees Fahrenheit (200 Celsius).

2. Prepare cake mix batter according to directions on the box.

3. Place butter and sugar in a microwavable bowl. Microwave on high setting for 20 second intervals, stirring in between, until melted.

4. Evenly distribute the mixture among 12 muffin cups.

5. Place 3-4 pineapple pieces in each muffin cup.

6. Pour cake batter into muffin cups, filling 2/3 of the way.

7. Bake until cupcakes pass the 'clean toothpick test,' about 15 minutes.

8. Serve upside down. Enjoy!

Mini Pumpkin Pie

These sweet little tarts are fun served warm with some ice cream. Measurements will yield 24 individual pumpkin pies.

Ingredients:

- 3 Large Eggs

- 2 Pie Crust Sheets

- 1 Cup Pumpkin, Canned

- 8 Oz. Cream Cheese

- 1/2 Cup White Granulated Sugar

- 1 Tsp. Vanilla

- 1 Tsp. Pumpkin Pie Spice

Cookware:

Muffin/Cupcake Tin, 4" (10 cm) Round cookie Cutter, Medium Mixing Bowl

Directions:

1. Preheat oven to 350 degrees Fahrenheit (175 Celsius).

2. Lay out the pie crust sheets and cut out 12 circles with the cookie cutter.

3. Press each dough circle into a muffin cup, pressing it up against the walls.

4. Separate 1 egg – you will only need the egg white.

5. Apply egg white to the top edge of each mini pie shell

6. In a medium mixing bowl, mix remaining ingredients until well blended.

7. Distribute mixture among 24 muffin cups.

8. Bake until edges of pie crusts are golden brown, about 12-15 minutes

9. Cool on a rack before refrigerating.

10. As a general rule, the longer cheesecake is refrigerated, the denser the texture. They can be eaten right away, but will be richer if refrigerated for several hours.

Handy and Hardy Shepherd's Pies

These are very filling and can be flash frozen to eat later on. Feel free to adjust the ground beef and vegetable measurements to suit your family's tastes. I find this to be a very comfort food-esque, which is great for wet or cold days. Measurements yield 6 pies.

Ingredients:

- 1 Lb. (455 g) Ground Beef, 80/20 or Leaner, Cooked and Drained.

- 2 Cups Mixed Veggies

- 3 Cups Mashed Potatoes

- 1 Gravy Packet

- 8 Oz. Cream Cheese

- 1 Cup Cheddar Cheese, Shredded

- 2 Cloves Garlic, Crushed

Cookware:

Muffin/Cupcake Tin, Medium Mixing Bowl

Directions:

1. Preheat oven to 375 degrees Fahrenheit (190 Celsius).

2. Cook up the mashed potatoes with cream cheese, 1/4 cup shredded cheese and garlic cloves.

3. Combine cooked ground beef and vegetables (make certain veggies are thawed, if using frozen) in mixing bowl.

4. Evenly distribute beef and veggie mixture among muffin cups.

5. Evenly distribute mashed potatoes on top.

6. Top with remaining cheese.

7. Bake 20 minutes, just long enough for the flavors to merge and the cheese to melt.

8. Serve warm and refrigerate any leftovers.

Piping Hot Dippin' Burgers

These remind me of those steamed mini burgers that some fast food places have been serving lately. I like to make lots of these for when my friends come over to watch sporting events. My husband loves them because he can dip them in ketchup or a 'special sauce' mixture as he eats.

Ingredients:

- 24 Oz. (680 g) Ground Beef, 80/20 or Better, Cooked and Drained

- 1 Canister Prepared Biscuits, 8-Count

- 1 Large Egg

- 1/2 Cup Ketchup or BBQ Sauce

- 1/3 Cup Relish

- 2 Tbsps. Mustard

- 4 Oz. Cream Cheese

- 1 Tsp. Water

- 1 Dash Onion Powder

- 1 Dash Salt

- 1 Pinch Black Pepper

- Optional: 2 Tsps. Sesame Seeds, for Garnish.

Cookware:

Muffin/Cupcake Tin, Saucepan

Directions:

1. Preheat oven to 350 degrees Fahrenheit (175 Celsius).

2. Grease muffin/cupcake tin.

3. In a saucepan over medium heat, stir together the cooked ground beef, cream cheese, ketchup/BBQ sauce, onion powder, salt and pepper until cheese is melted, about 5 minutes.

4. Split raw biscuits in half, for a total of 8 pieces of dough.

5. Press 4 of the biscuit halves into muffin cups, pressing up the sides and creating a well in the center of each. Reserve remaining halves for later.

6. Evenly distribute ground beef mixture into the pressed biscuits.

7. Top each one with a biscuit half, pressing on the edges to seal.

8. In small mixing bowl, mix egg and water.

9. Brush the tops with the egg mixture for a lovely golden color when baked.

10. Sprinkle sesame seeds on top to simulate the appearance of a burger bun.

11. Bake until golden brown, about 15-20 minutes.

12. Cool before serving, the centers will be piping hot. Refrigerate leftovers.

Mini Turkey Meatloaf

I was looking for an alternative to red meat when I came upon this tasty use for ground turkey. You may want to dress up the flavor a little more with your own favorite spices. I find that two of these with a side item make for a good dinner and can be flash frozen for eating later in the week.

Ingredients:

- 1 Lb. (455 G) Ground Turkey, Lean

- 2 Cups Carrots, Chopped

- 1-1/2 Cups Green Onions, Chopped

- 1 Large Egg

- 1 Green Bell Pepper, Chopped

- 1/2 Cup Uncooked Couscous

- 1/2 Cup Barbecue Sauce

- 2 Tablespoons Worcestershire Sauce

- 1 Tbsp. Mustard

- 1 Dash Salt

- 1 Dash Pepper

- Optional: Basil, to Taste.

Cookware:

Muffin/Cupcake Tin, Food Processor, Large Mixing Bowl

Directions:

1. Preheat oven to 400 degrees Fahrenheit (200 Celsius).

2. Grease muffin/cupcake tin.

3. Place vegetables in a food processor and combine together. Leave a little chunky for added texture, or shop finely for a smoother bite.

4. In a large mixing bowl, mix ground turkey (it will cook in the oven) with vegetable mixture and remaining ingredients (except BBQ sauce).

5. Fill muffin cups 3/4 of the way with mixture.

6. Top with 1 Tsp. BBQ sauce.

7. Bake until internal temperature reaches 160 degrees Fahrenheit (70 Celsius), about 25 minutes.

8. Center will be extremely hot, allow to cool before eating. Refrigerate leftovers.

Choco-Nana Bread Pudding

These cook up fairly quickly and satisfy the need for a warm dessert. The muffin-sized cups make good portions and prevent overeating, which is easy when something combines my three favorite things: chocolate, bananas and bread. Yields 12 cups.

Ingredients:

- 10 Slices Of White Bread, Lightly Toasted

- 3 Bananas, Sliced

- 2 Large Eggs

- 1 Cup Milk

- 9 Oz Milk Chocolate (Chips Or Broken-Up Bars)

- 2 Tbsps. Light Brown Sugar

- 1 Tsp. Butter

- 2 Tsps. Vanilla

Cookware:

Muffin/Cupcake Tin, Skillet, Large Mixing Bowl

Directions:

1. Preheat oven to 350 degrees Fahrenheit (175 Celsius).

2. Grease muffin/cupcake tin or use paper liners.

3. In skillet, melt butter and sugar, stirring together.

4. Place banana slices in skillet and cook for about three minutes. This will caramelize them. Take the skillet off of the heat and cool.

5. In a large mixing bowl, whisk together eggs, milk and vanilla.

6. Cut crusts off of bread and cut into fourths.

7. Soak the bread in the egg mixture for 10 minutes.

8. Stir bananas and chocolate into mixture.

9. Evenly distribute the chocolate-banana-bead mixture into muffin cups.

10. Bake until tops are golden brown, about 25 minutes.

Book Three: Muffin Tin Cuisine

Mac n Cheese Mouthfuls

Macaroni and cheese is done so many ways that it can be hard to pick a recipe that will work for everyone. This one is creamy, has more depth than processed cheese and has cheesy crunch from an oven that many people want.

Ingredients:

- 2 Cups Elbow Macaroni

- 1-1/2 Cups Cheddar, Shredded

- 1-1/2 Cups Mozzarella, Shredded

- 1 Egg, Beaten

- 1 Cup Milk

- 1/2 Cup Italian Bread Crumbs

- 1 Tbsp. Butter

- 2 Tsps. Olive Oil

- 1 Dash Salt

Cookware:

Muffin Tin/Cupcake Tin, Small Mixing Bowl, Pot

Directions:

1. Preheat oven to 350 degrees Fahrenheit (177 Celsius).

2. Grease muffin tin or use paper liners.

3. Mix together bread crumbs, olive oil and salt in a small mixing bowl.

4. Bring pot of water with a dash of salt to a boil. Add elbow macaroni and cook for 8 minutes.

5. Drain pasta and return it to the pot.

6. Add butter and beaten egg to the pot, stirring constantly until all the pasta is coated.

7. Add 1 cup of the cheddar cheese and all of the mozzarella cheese. Stir constantly for one minute.

8. Disperse the pasta mixture across 12 muffin cups.

9. Spoon the bread crumb mixture on top of pasta cups, and then sprinkle remaining 1/2 cup cheddar on top.

10. Bake until the tops are nicely browned, about 30 minutes.

11. Allow them to cool in the pan for about 5 minutes. They will not hold their shape otherwise.

12. Serve warm or reheat later.

Danish Delights

I make these every other Sunday to go with the family's breakfast. They are so easy to make that you probably won't even need to look at the recipe again when you make it a second time.

Everything comes prepackaged, except for the cream cheese mixture. Straight up cream cheese is not sweet enough, but adding that something extra is easy. Try these when you have about 15 minutes to spare. They're hot, sweet and filling. Makes 8.

Ingredients:

- 1 8-Count Canister of Crescent Rolls

- 6 Oz. (170 g) Cream Cheese

- 1/4 Cup Confectioner's Sugar

- 1 Dash Vanilla

- 1 Egg Yolk

- 6 Tbsp. Strawberry Jam (any jam will work)

Cookware:

Muffin Tin/Cupcake Tin, Medium Mixing Bowl

Directions:

1. Preheat oven to 400 degrees Fahrenheit (204 Celsius).

2. Grease muffin tin. Paper liners will be a little difficult to work with here.

3. Unwrap crescent rolls.

4. Starting with the bottom center of a muffin cup, cover the metal surface with the crescent roll. It works best if you roll it around from that bottom center point.

5. In a medium mixing bowl, combine all remaining ingredients except the jam.

6. Spoon the mixture evenly among all of the muffin cups, and then press an indentation in the middle with the back of a spoon.

7. Spoon some jam into the indentations.

8. Bake until filling is set and the dough is golden brown, about 10 minutes.

Pancake Fruit Cups

These warm, handheld breakfast bites of heaven are amazing. Instead of dousing pancakes in syrup, you get to enjoy them infused with fruit and a glaze.

Yes, you can use a box of pancake mix for this, but do not use the kind that only needs water. Pick one out that requires milk, then add yogurt instead of milk. Try this from-scratch recipe for a fluffier, full-bodied pancake. Makes 12.

Ingredients:

Pancake

- 2/3 Cup Unbleached All-Purpose Flour

- 2/3 Cup Of Fruit, Diced (think peaches, pears, berries)

- 1/3 Cup Whole Wheat Flour

- 1/4 Cup Plain Yogurt

- 4 Eggs

- 2 Tbsps. Butter, Melted

- 1 Tbsp .Ground Flaxseed

- 1 Tbsp. Wheat Germ

- 1 Dash Cinnamon

Fruit Sauce

- 2/3 Cup Of Fruit, Diced (same used above)

- 2 Tsp. White Granulated Sugar

- 3 Tbsp Water

Cookware:

Muffin/Cupcake Tin, Large Mixing Bowl, Medium Mixing Bowl, Saucepan

Directions:

Pancake Cupcakes

9. Preheat oven to 400 degrees Fahrenheit (204 Celsius).

10. Grease muffin tins or insert paper liners.

11. In a large mixing bowl, combine all of the dry ingredients.

12. In a medium mixing bowl, gently combine remaining ingredients in the 'pancake' section of the ingredients list.

13. Carefully fold the wet mixture into the large bowl of dry ingredients.

14. Disperse the batter evenly among 12 muffin cups.

15. Bake until they can path a clean toothpick test, about 15 minutes.

Fruit Sauce

16. Combine all of the ingredients for the sauce in a saucepan over medium heat.

17. Cook for about 5-6 minutes, stirring constantly.

18. Use a hand beater, immersion blender or elbow grease and whatever you use to mash potatoes to crush the fruit and blend it with the sugary water. Leave it a little chunky.

19. Spoon some sauce over the fresh pancake cupcakes.

20. Serve warm and enjoy!

Yogurt-Filled Granola Cups

These taste just like granola bars, but are shaped into cups that are perfect for yogurt. I make lots of the cups and store them in a container in the fridge to make my morning yogurt more nutritious. Makes 12.

Ingredients:

- 1-1/4 Cups Rolled Oats (not instant)

- 1 Cup Yogurt (pick your favorite!)

- 1 Large Egg

- 1/3 Cup Wheat Germ

- 1/2 Cup Chopped Nuts (any kind)

- 1/2 Cup Raisins (or dried cranberries)

- 1/2 Cup Chopped Dried Fruit (any)

- 1/2 Cup Honey

- 1/4 Cup Coconut Oil, Melted (this stuff is amazing)

- 1/2 Tbsp. Cinnamon

- 1 Dash Allspice

- 1 Dash Teaspoon Salt

- 1 Tsp. Lemon Zest

Cookware:

Muffin/Cupcake Tin, 2 Large Mixing Bowls. 1 Medium Mixing Bowl

Directions:

1. Preheat oven to 350 degrees Fahrenheit (177 Celsius).

2. In a large mixing bowl, combine oats, wheat germ, nuts, dried fruits, lemon zest, and spices.

3. In the other large mixing bowl, beat egg.

4. Stir honey and coconut oil into the beaten egg.

5. Slowly add wet ingredients to dry and combine.

6. Split up the mixture among 12 muffin cups. Wet your finger and press the mixture up the sides until they resemble small pie crusts.

7. Bake until edges begin to turn golden brown, about 20 minutes.

8. Allow to cool for 5 minutes before removing from muffin tin.

9. Dollop yogurt into each cup and serve immediately.

Maple Sausage Pancake Bites

These fluffy pancake bites have the savory taste and texture of sausage and the sweet richness of maple syrup. Makes 12.

Ingredients:

- 1 Cup Pancake Mix (the 'just add water' kind)

- 2/3 Cup Half and Half

- 1/2 Cup Maple Syrup

- 1 Tbsp. Light Brown Sugar

- 1/2 Cup Cooked Sausage (I use the fully-cooked kind that just need to be heated), Crumbled

- Optional: Go a little crazy and get 1/4 Cup blueberries! They work better if chilled for at least 30 minutes.

Cookware:

Muffin Tin/Cupcake Tin, Large Mixing Bowl

Directions:

1. Preheat oven to 350 degrees Fahrenheit (177 Celsius).

2. Grease muffin tin or use paper liners.

3. In a large mixing bowl, mix everything except syrup until smooth.

4. Add syrup a little bit at a time and blend into the mixture.

5. Divide mixture among 12 muffin cups.

6. Sprinkle the sausage among the muffin cups.

7. Optional: Disperse a few blueberries here and there.

8. Bake until the muffin centers are set and the edges are golden, about 15 minutes.

9. Serve warm.

PB&J Muffins

These are handy peanut butter and jelly muffins that you can keep around all of the time for snack attacks. It has all of the goodness of a pb&j sandwich, but you can make these ahead of time and not worry about stale bread!

Ingredients:

- 1 Cup Pancake Mix (and ingredients required to prepare it on the back of the box)

- 3/4 Cup Creamy Peanut Butter

- 3/4 Cup Jelly (any)

Cookware:

Muffin Tin/Cupcake Tin, Large Mixing Bowl

Directions:

1. Preheat oven to 350 degrees Fahrenheit (177 Celsius).

2. Grease muffin tin or use paper liners.

3. Prepare pancake mix according to instructions on the box.

4. Mix in 3/4 Cup of creamy peanut butter until well blended.

5. Fill the muffin cups 1/3 of the way with batter mixture.

6. Spoon one tablespoon of jelly into each muffin cup.

7. Fill muffin cups with remaining batter, pouring slowly.

8. Bake for 10-15 minutes, until the centers have set.

Mashed Potato Bake

This is a wonderful way to cut down on cooking time and distribute heat evenly with a potato bake. The heated ingredients will release their flavors and blend more easily with each other.

Ingredients:

- 2-1/2 Lbs. (1.36 kg) Potatoes, Cooked and Mashed

- 1 Cup Half and Half

- 2 Tbsp. Butter

- 1 Garlic Clove, Mashed

- Optional: 1/2 Cup of flavor bits to mix in, such as chives, bacon, etc.

Cookware:

Muffin Tin/Cupcake Tin, Pot

Directions:

1. Preheat oven to 375 degrees Fahrenheit (191 Celsius).
2. Grease the muffin tin or use paper liners.
3. Mix mashed potatoes with butter, half and half and garlic.
4. Add optional flavor bits to taste and mix well.

5. Distribute mashed potato mixture evenly among muffin cups.

6. With a fork, create a pattern by running the teeth across the top in one direction.

7. Bake uncovered until the tops are golden brown and set, about 20-30 minutes.

8. Allow them to cool for several minutes and use a butter knife to remove from the tin.

Calzones

These are smaller than your typical restaurant calzone and look great on a plate. You can make lots of them at once thanks to the muffin tin and flash freeze them in freezer bags to reheat for later. Makes 8.

Ingredients:

- 8 Pizza Dough Balls, 1-1/2 Inch (3.8 Cm) Diameter
- 2 Sausages, Diced
- 2 Cloves Of Garlic
- 1 Egg

- 1/2 Lb. (227 G) Baby Spinach

- 1/2 Cup Ricotta

- 1/2 Cup Mozzarella

- 1/2 Cup Sweet Spaghetti Or Marinara Sauce

- 2 Tbsps Olive Oil

- 1 Tbsp. Cream

Cookware:

Muffin Tin/Cupcake Tin, Frying Pan, Small Mixing Bowl

Directions:

1. Preheat oven to 375 degrees Fahrenheit (191 Celsius).

2. Grease the muffin tin well.

3. Roll the dough balls out into flat circles about 1/4"(6.35 mm) thick with a 5" (12.7 cm) diameter.

4. Cook sausage with garlic and olive oil over medium in in a frying pan, and then add baby spinach. Cook until the greens have wilted.

5. Press the dough circles into the muffin cups.

6. Spoon 1 tbsp. of sauce into the calzone, then 2 tbsps. sausage and spinach.

7. Add 1 tbsp. ricotta, then one tbsp. mozzarella.

8. Seal the calzone shut by pinching the dough together on top.

9. In a small mixing bowl, combine the egg and milk to create an egg wash. Brush the exposed dough with it.

10. Bake until golden brown, about 15-20 minutes. Be careful when serving immediately, they are piping hot!

Bacon-Wrapped Egg Scramble

It may not sound special, but it is very pretty to look at and is easy to customize. The bacon cooks right into the cheesy eggs and makes the whole thing taste amazing. The bacon ribbon around the golden-colored scrambled eggs look as good as they taste. Makes 6.

Ingredients:

- 6 Eggs, Beaten

- 6 Strips of Uncooked Bacon

- 1/2 Cup Cheese (any)

- Salt And Pepper to Taste

Cookware:

Muffin Tin/Cupcake Tin, Medium Mixing Bowl

1. Preheat oven to 350 degrees Fahrenheit (177 Celsius).

2. Grease muffin tin or use easy-release paper liners. Normal paper liners will stick to the egg after cooking.

3. In a medium mixing bowl, combine eggs, cheese and seasonings.

4. Line each muffin cup's walls with one bacon strip. Make sure it goes around the whole circumference of the cup.

5. Carefully pour in the egg mixture, trying not to displace the bacon, until the cups are 3/4 full.

6. Bake for about 30 minutes, or until eggs are done, but not rubbery.

7. Remove from the tin and set on a plate. It is as pretty to look at as it is delicious.

No-Bake Mini Cheesecakes

I love making (and eating) cheesecake, but I don't love being a slave to the cooking process all day. These are perfect for get-togethers, family dinners and can be made days ahead of time. Makes 12.

Ingredients:

- 1 Cup Graham Cracker Crumbs

- 6 Oz (179 G) Cream Cheese, Softened

- 2/3 Cup Ricotta Cheese

- 2/3 Cup Nuts (any), Finely Chopped

- 1/3 Cup Maple Syrup

- 2 Tbsps. White Granulated Sugar

- 1 Dash Vanilla Extract

Cookware:

Muffin Tin/Cupcake Tin, 2 Large Mixing Bowls

Directions:

1. Line a muffin tin with paper liners.

2. In a large mixing bowl, combine graham crackers crumbs, nuts and syrup.

3. In another large mixing bowl, combine remaining ingredients until smooth. Make sure that it is free of any lumps.

4. Divide the crumb mixture among 12 muffin cups and press it down against the bottom, making the crust as dense as possible.

5. Distribute the cheese mixture evenly among the muffin cups.

6. Chill overnight for a firm and decadent personal-size dessert. Garnish with any sauces or fruits that you would like.

Eggplant Parmesan

This great eggplant parmesan variant is everything that you could ask for, but easier to serve, store and reheat. It has the texture, the savory flavors and all of the satisfaction of the Italian classic. Makes 6.

Ingredients:

- 1-1/2 Cups Fire-Roasted Tomatoes, Crushed

- 1 Lb. (454 g) Eggplant, Sliced into 18 Rounds 1/4" (6.4 mm) thick.

- 1 Cup Panko Bread Crumbs

- 1 Cup Broccoletti (Rapini) Sliced

- 6 Oz. (170 G) Mozzarella, Shredded

- 1/3 Cup Basil Leaves

- 4 Oz (113g) Parmesan, Grated

- 1 Egg, Beaten with 1 Tbsp. Water

- 2 Garlic Cloves, Minced

- 1 Tbsp. Red Wine Vinegar

- 1 Dash Red Pepper Flakes

- 1 Pinch Oregano

- Salt And Pepper To Taste

Cookware:

Jumbo Muffin Tin, Blender/Food Processor, 2 Shallow Bowls or Containers, Baking Sheet, Parchment Paper

Directions:

1. Preheat oven to 375 degrees Fahrenheit (191 Celsius).

2. Grease the muffin tin with a nonstick spray.

3. Puree crushed tomatoes in a food processor or blender. Combine with red wine vinegar, garlic, basil, red pepper flakes, salt and pepper. Pour into a shallow container for dredging.

4. In a shallow bowl or container, combine beaten egg with panko, 2 oz. grated parmesan, oregano, and salt and pepper.

5. If necessary, trim the eggplant rounds so that they can fit in the muffin tin.

6. Line a baking sheet with parchment paper.

7. Dip the eggplant rounds in the egg mixture, then dredge them in bread crumbs. Place on the baking sheet.

8. Bake for 15 minutes, then flip them over and cook for another 15.

9. Time to assemble the eggplant parmesan! Place one toasted eggplant round in 6 muffin cups.

10. Top with 1-1/2 tbsps. sauce, then 1-1/2 mozzarella, and then rapini.

11. Top all this with another toasted eggplant round, then 1-1/2 tbsps. tomato sauce, then 1-1/2 tbsps. mozzarella, then the remaining rapini.

12. Now the last layer: toasted eggplant round, 1-1/2 tbsps. tomato sauce and 1-1/2 tbsps. mozzarella.

13. Bake until the cheese melts, about 10 minutes.

14. Cool for a few minutes before serving. Refrigerate leftovers.

Ham and Egg Breakfast

Nothing is more quintessential than ham and eggs. Get rid of the carbs completely with this one and feed a household without having to cook just one or two eggs at a time. This recipe can be easily double or tripled. Depending on how you like your eggs, you may need to eat this on a plate with a fork and knife. Makes 6.

Ingredients:

- 6 Eggs

- 6 Round Slices of Ham

- 1/4 Cup Cheese (any), Grated

- Optional 1/4 Cup Scallions, Sliced

- Salt and Pepper to Taste

- Optional: A touch of Old Bay seasoning or cayenne pepper.

Cookware:

Muffin Tin/Cupcake Tin

Directions:

1. Preheat oven to 400 degrees Fahrenheit (204 Celsius).

2. Heavily coat the muffin tin with nonstick coating or line with a paper liner.

3. Place a slice of ham into each muffin cup, making sure it covers all of the metal surface.

4. Crack an egg in the center of each muffin cup. It helps to crack the egg open as close as possible.

5. Season egg with salt and pepper (and optional seasonings) to taste.

6. Bake for 12 minutes, until the whites are firm.

7. Immediately after removing from the oven, sprinkle on cheese and green onions.

8. Serve as soon as the cheese starts to melt (which should be almost right away).

Fish Tacos

The freshness of a fish taco made with sweet mangos, rich avocados and tangy green onions can take any ordinary day and make it something special. A touch of chipotle pepper in adobe sauce with cumin really kicks this dish into high gear. The muffin cup preparation technique gives it a great specialty look. Serves 6.

Ingredients:

- 6 (5-Inch) Corn Tortillas (corn hardens better than flour in the oven)

- 1½ Cups Lettuce, Shredded (1 lettuce head will yield about 6 cups)

- 1 Mango, Cubed

- 1 Avocado, Cubed

- 12 Oz. (340 G) Tilapia, Washed and Cubed

- 1/2 Cup Greek Yogurt, Plain

- 1/3 Cup Cilantro

- 2 Green Onions, Sliced Thin

- 2 Tbsps. Lime

- 1 Tsp. Chipotle Pepper In Adobo Sauce

  (these are available canned)

- 1 Dash Salt

- 1 Dash Paprika

- 1 Dash Ground Cumin

- 1 Pinch Pepper

- Zest Of 1 Lime

- Oil Spray or 2 Tbsps Oil and Brush

Cookware:

Muffin Tin/Cupcake Tin, Microwave-Safe Plate, 1 Glass (for pressing – it has to be able to fit in a muffin cup), Medium Mixing Bowl, 2 Small Mixing Bowl

Directions:

9. On a microwave-safe plate, stack the tortilla shells and cook for 25 seconds on high power.

10. Pick up a tortilla and spray both sides with oil, then press it into a muffin cup.

11. Use a glass to press the tortilla and make it conform to the muffin cup.

12. Repeat steps 2 and 3 with all the tortillas.

13. Preheat oven to 375 degrees Fahrenheit (191 Celsius).

14. Divide the lettuce among the muffin cups.

15. In a medium mixing bowl, combine salt, pepper, paprika, cumin and lime zest. Toss cubed tilapia in the mixture and divide among tortilla cups.

16. Bake for 15 minutes, until fish is cooked.

17. In a small mixing bowl, combine 1 tbsp. lime juice, green onions, cubed mango, cubed avocado, cilantro and salt to taste.

18. In another small mixing bowl, combine yogurt, chipotle pepper, and lime juice.

19. Top cooked fish tacos with mango mixture and a dollop of spicy yogurt.

20. Serve warm .

French Toast Bowls

French toast is always great, but especially when they acts as bowls for caramelized fruits, fresh glazes and smooth yogurt.

Ingredients:

- 6 Bread Slices (normal thickness, do not use Texas toast)

- 4 Eggs, Beaten

- 2-3/4 Cups Fruit (peaches work great), Diced

- 1/2 Cup Greek Yogurt, Plain

- 2 Tsps. Milk or Half And Half

- 2 Tbsps. White Granulated Sugar

- 1 Tbsp. Lemon Juice

- 2 Dashes Cinnamon

- 1 Dash Vanilla Extract

- 1 Pinch Nutmeg

Cookware:

Muffin Tin/Cupcake Tin, Flat Container (for soaking bread), Large Mixing Bowl, Skillet, Small Mixing Bowl

Directions:

1. Preheat oven to 375 degrees Fahrenheit (191 Celsius).

2. Flatten the bread to 1/4" (6.35 mm) thickness by rolling a can over it or using a rolling pin.

3. In a flat container or bowl, beat eggs, sugar, milk (or half and half), cinnamon and nutmeg together.

4. Soak the bread slices in the mixture one at a time, about 10 seconds per side.

5. Press each one into a muffin cup, forming a bowl shape.

6. Bake until the bread becomes crisp, about 10-14 minutes.

7. While the French toast bowl is baking, toss together the remaining ingredients in a large mixing bowl.

8. Heat this mixture in a skillet for about 5 minutes. This will create softened fruit and sweet syrup.

9. In a small bowl, combine yogurt and vanilla.

10. When the French toast bowls are ready, divide the fruit among them and then top with yogurt.

Chocolate Nut Berry Cups

These look and taste like an expensive trip to a specialty candy shop. Use fresh fruits, skip the cheap chocolate and try contrasting colors to stimulate your eyes as well as your taste buds. White chocolate and raspberries look great together.

Ingredients:

- 1 Cup Cashews, Unsalted And Raw

- 2/3 Cup Blueberries

- 2/3 Cup Raspberries

- 6 Oz. (170 g) Chocolate Chips (milk chocolate, white chocolate, etc., it's up to you)

- 1 Dash vanilla extract

Cookware:

Muffin Tin/Cupcake Tin, Small Bowl, Blender, Small Saucepan

Directions:

1. Soak cashews in water for two hours.

2. Transfer soaked cashews into a blender or food processor, and then add enough water to cover them.

3. Process until they become a smooth mixture.

4. Line muffin tin with paper liners.

5. Evenly divide berries among muffin cups.

6. In a saucepan over low heat, stir together chocolate chips, cashews and vanilla until well blended.

7. Carefully pour the mixture into the muffin cups.

8. Place muffin tin in freezer for several hours, until chocolate is solid.

9. Avoid freezer burn by unmolding chocolates and storing them in a plastic bag.

Chicken Alfredo Pasta Bowl

Make your own bread bowls at home and save a lot of money in the process. These are carbohydrate heavy, but most comfort foods are. Create these indulgent dinner portions in under 30 minutes. Makes 8.

Ingredients:

- 2 cups chicken, cooked and chopped

- 1 8-Count Canister Buttermilk Biscuits

- 1 cup penne pasta, cooked

- 1/2 cup Parmesan, shredded

- 15 Oz. (444 mL) Alfredo Sauce

- 9 Oz (255 g) Spinach

Cookware:

Muffin Tin/Cupcake Tin, Large Mixing Bowl

Directions:

1. Preheat oven to 350 degrees Fahrenheit (177 Celsius).

2. In a large mixing bowl, combine chicken, sauce and spinach.

3. Flatten out biscuits and press into muffin tin, covering the sides a well as the bottom.

4. Distribute chicken mixture among muffin cups.

5. Sprinkle cheese on top of each one.

6. Bake until biscuits are golden brown, about 25-30 minutes.

Jalapeno Cheddar Appetizers

Whether you making snacks to watch a big game, enjoy a movie night at home or are looking for party snack ideas, these are sure to be a hit. Easy and satisfying, these cheddar and jalapeno snacks pack just enough punch for any appetizer aficionado. Makes 6.

Ingredients:

- 6 Wonton Wrappers

- 4 Oz. (113 g) Cream Cheese, Softened

- 1/2 Cup Cheddar Cheese, Shredded

- 2 Jalapeno Peppers

- 1 Dash Hot Pepper Sauce

Cookware:

Muffin Tin/Cupcake Tin

Directions:

1. Preheat oven to 350 degrees Fahrenheit (177 Celsius).

2. Lightly grease the muffin tin.

3. Place one wonton wrapper into each cup.

4. Remove seeds from jalapenos and dice them.

5. In a medium mixing bowl, combine cream cheese, cheddar cheese, hot sauce and jalapenos.

6. Spoon the cheese mixture into the wonton wrappers.

7. Bake until the edges of the wonton wrappers turn golden brown, about 15-20 minutes.

Mini Apple Pies

There really is no underestimating the sweet perfection of a warm slice of apple pie. This celebrated dessert makes a great mini pie, with every bit as much texture and taste as its bigger version. This version is just the right size for a crowning scoop of vanilla ice cream. Makes 6.

Ingredients:

- 2 Medium Apples, Peeled and Diced

- Pie Crust Dough

- 1/4 Cup White Granulated Sugar

- 1/4 Cup Light Brown Sugar

- 1 Tbsp. Flour

- 1 Dash Cinnamon

- 1 Dash Vanilla

- 1 Pinch Nutmeg

- 1 Pinch Salt

Cookware:

Muffin Tin/Cupcake Tin, Medium Mixing Bowl, 5" (12.7 cm) Round Cookie Cutter, Baking Sheet

Directions:

1. In a medium mixing bowl, combine brown sugar, flour, nutmeg, cinnamon and vanilla.

2. Toss apples in the sugar mixture.

3. Cut 5" (12.7 cm) circles out of the pie dough and press them into the muffin cups. Do not grease the muffin tin, pie dough has enough butter built in.

4. Fill the muffin cups 3/4 of the way with apples.

5. You can be creative with the top pastry part of the pie. Cut strips and cross them on top, or cut out a circle an opening (to vent the cooking apples) and place on top.

6. Place the muffin tin on a baking sheet (not using a baking sheet will result in the bottoms

of the pie burning) and bake until the tops start to brown, about 35-40 minutes.

7. Allow them to cool for a few minutes before gently removing them from the tin with a knife.

Cover images used through license with

stockfreeimages.com

Made in the USA
San Bernardino, CA
03 April 2015